For all the Happy Home School students and staff
from the past, present, and future . . .
–R.F.

To Karim Nasr,
who taught me the names of colors.
–H.H.

Milloo's Mind
Text copyright © 2023 by Reem Faruqi
Illustrations copyright © 2023 by Hoda Hadadi
Photo on p. 36 courtesy of Reem Faruqi
All rights reserved. Manufactured in Italy.
No part of this book may be used or reproduced in any manner whatsoever
without written permission except in the case of brief quotations embodied in critical
articles and reviews. For information address HarperCollins Children's Books,
a division of HarperCollins Publishers, 195 Broadway, New York, NY 10007.
www.harpercollinschildrens.com

Library of Congress Control Number: 2022930101

ISBN 978-0-06-305661-9

The artist used paper collage to create the illustrations for this book.
Typography by Rachel Zegar
22 23 24 25 26 RTLO 10 9 8 7 6 5 4 3 2 1
❖
First Edition

Milloo's Mind

THE STORY OF MARYAM FARUQI, TRAILBLAZER FOR WOMEN'S EDUCATION

Written by **Reem Faruqi**   Illustrated by **Hoda Hadadi**

HARPER
An Imprint of HarperCollinsPublishers

As the sun swallowed the last
part of the night, children in Poona,
India, rubbed sleep from their eyes.
   Not Milloo.
   Milloo woke up early to read.
   When she read, her thoughts danced, her
mind breathed, and her heart hummed.

"Milloo! Time for school!" yelled her brothers.

Milloo snaked past the sabzi wala,

cha-chaed past
the chai wala,

danced through the dusty alleys,

all the way to school.

Although Milloo knew every
answer, she didn't raise her hand.
She looked down at the floor.

One day Milloo's teacher didn't come.

Children drew on the chalkboard.

Children stood on chairs.
Children threw paper airplanes.

Milloo wanted to read, but it was too noisy.

She closed her book.
SNAP!

She put her hands on her hips. She stomped to the front of the class. She whistled loudly.

"Enough is enough!"

Milloo grabbed a piece of chalk and began to teach her class.

When the teacher returned, Milloo raised her hand the highest.

Milloo spoke the loudest.

Because Milloo decided she wanted to be a teacher.

When Milloo finished fifth grade, her parents told her: "You don't need to go to school anymore. You need to stay home like other girls and do housework." It was 1930, and this is what was expected of her.

"How will I become a teacher if I don't finish school?" wailed Milloo.

The whole summer, Milloo wrote letters to her parents.

But only her father could read them because her mother never went to school.

Her mother finally said, "If you're going to keep on learning, you should learn English too . . ."

Milloo only spoke Urdu, like her parents.

But she didn't care, as long as she could go back to school.

On the first day of sixth grade, Milloo yelled to her brothers, "Time for school!"

Milloo spun past the samosa wala,

cha-chaed past the chutney wala,

tiptoed past
the tonga wala,

all the way to her new school.

SCHOOL

But when she got to her classroom . . .
the children were tiny.
They wrote nonsense.
They talked gibberish.

SCHOOL
IS OPEN
SCHOOL
IS close

I am go
home
and eat
my lunch
Here is

Milloo's new teacher said, "We've put you
back in third grade to learn English . . ."
Milloo's cheeks felt hot.
She made her feet move to her desk.
One step after the other.

Some children stared at her.
Some children laughed at her.
Some children stuck their tongues out at her.
But Milloo kept her eyes on her new teacher.

At home, Milloo whispered, *"Enough is enough!"*

Every morning, Milloo got up early.

She sounded out English letters.

KNOWLEDGE

She practiced writing new words.
Slowly, her heart started to hum again.

Milloo went on to high school *and* college. She graduated
with the highest grades.

Milloo bought books, sharpened pencils, and wrote lesson
plans, dreaming of her own classroom.

Then Milloo got married. Her life changed.
She packed her teaching bag for work, but
her husband asked her to stay home instead.

But when Milloo cooked, her
head stewed, and when she sewed,
her mind got tangled.

Milloo went for a walk. She noticed girls
scrubbing pots, sweeping dusty floors, and
hanging up laundry . . . girls who should be going
to school.

Milloo stopped her walk, put her hands on her
hips, and headed to the bazaar.

"Enough is enough!"

Milloo bought chairs and tables and put them in her kitchen.
She bought swings and a seesaw and put them in her backyard.
She bought a piano and put it in her family room.
She bought juice and lots of cookies.
She opened her doors wide and soon enough . . .
Children were singing songs in the family room.
Children were reading rhymes in the dining room.
Children were tracing trapezoids in the kitchen.

Milloo's husband looked around . . .
"Enough is enough!" he said.

So Milloo opened a school.
Children filled every classroom.

Milloo opened another school.   And another.   And another.

Because of Milloo's dream, thousands of girls went to school.

And just as the moon swallowed
the last part of the day, and the clouds
floated to sleep, Milloo's students in
Karachi, Pakistan, stayed awake reading.
Their thoughts danced, their minds
breathed, and their hearts hummed.

GLOSSARY

sabzi wala: vegetable seller

chai wala: tea seller

Urdu: Pakistani language

samosa wala: samosa seller. A samosa is
a fried savory triangular pastry containing
spiced vegetables or meat.

tonga wala: tonga driver. A tonga is a light carriage drawn by a horse, used for transportation in India, Pakistan, and Bangladesh.

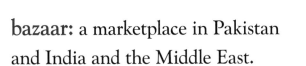

bazaar: a marketplace in Pakistan and India and the Middle East.

AUTHOR'S NOTE

My grandmother, **Maryam Faruqi** (December 13, 1920–April 9, 2012), affectionately called Milloo by her father, is famous for founding Happy Home Schools in Karachi, Pakistan. These schools are still thriving today. As a young child, she had a love for education. Many girls did not go on to middle or high school or college and instead stayed home. In fact, Maryam's older sister stayed home to help with the family and chores while Maryam fought to keep on staying in school. Maryam graduated at the top of her class from Bombay University in 1946. In her own words, she would say, "I never stood second." When she was featured in the newspaper for her accomplishments, many young men wrote to her asking for her hand in marriage. An educator at heart, she married the man with the neatest handwriting and most elegant Urdu language, my grandfather. After the Partition of India in 1947, the division that created two separate countries, India and Pakistan, Maryam moved to Karachi, Pakistan, with her husband and taught there. In Pakistan, she was trained by Maria Montessori.

When Maryam took a class for cooking and stitching, she said it was "a course in which I was least interested." Unfulfilled, she opened a school in her home: she said, "My happiness knew no bounds, as I wanted to use my education."

In 1960, Maryam Faruqi won the Fulbright scholarship to study educational administration and supervision in the United States, where she met and garlanded President John F. Kennedy.

She won scores of lifetime achievement awards, including the President's Award for Literacy (1987) as well as awards from the prime minister and the president of Pakistan. She educated thousands of students, students who have flourished in various professions in life.